WHALE WATCHING WITH A BOY AND A GOAT

Other books by the author:

POETRY
The Stone Spiral (Giant Steps, 1987, reprinted 1988)
Ten Letters to John Muir (Burbage Books, 1990)
Outcrops (Littlewood/Arc, 1991)
The Rope (Redbeck Press, 1996)
The Blue Bang Theory: New Nature Poetry (with John Sewell, Colin Sutherill and Diana Syder, Redbeck, 1997)

CRITICISM
Ted Hughes: A Critical Study (with Neil Roberts, Faber and Faber, 1981)
Green Voices: Understanding Contemporary Nature Poetry (Manchester University Press, 1995)

EDUCATION
Teaching A Level English Literature: A Student-Centred Approach (with John Brown, Routledge, 1989)

EDITING
John Muir: The Eight Wilderness-Discovery Books (Diadem, 1992)
Not Not Not Not Not Enough Oxygen and Other Plays by Caryl Churchill (with Gill Round, Longman, 1993)
Orogenic Zones: The First Five Years of the International Festival of Mountaineering Literature (with Rosie Smith, Bretton Hall, 1994)
John Muir: His Life and Letters and Other Writings (Bâton Wicks, 1996)
The Climbers' Club Centenary Journal (Climbers' Club, 1997)
The Literature of Nature: An International Sourcebook (UK chapters, with Patrick Murphy, Fitzroy Dearborn, 1998)

WHALE WATCHING WITH A BOY AND A GOAT

Terry Gifford

Terry Gifford (signature)

Red Beck Press
1998

Whale Watching with a Boy and a Goat
is published by:
Redbeck Press, 24 Aireville Road, Frizinghall,
Bradford, BD9 4HH.

Design and print by Tony Ward, Arc & Throstle
Press, Nanholme Mill, Shaw Wood Road,
Todmorden, Lancs. OL14 6DA.

Copyright © Terry Gifford 1998

Whale Watching with a Boy and a Goat
ISBN 0 946980 59 4

Redbeck Press acknowledges financial
assistance from Yorkshire & Humberside Arts

Acknowledgements are due to the following magazines, journals and books in which some of these poems were first published: *The Alpine Journal, Bête Noir, The Climbing Art* (USA), *The Climbers' Club Journal, The Himalayan Club Newsletter* (India), *Spokes, Staple*. 'Why it's not possible to slip into Bradford', was published in *Spirit of Bradford* ed. David Tipton and Nick Toczek, (Redbeck Press, 1997), 'Cairo' in the *PHARAS 96 Competition Winners' Anthology*, 'Summer Love' in *The Red Deer Anthology* (1991). Some of these poems also appeared in *The Blue Bang Theory: New Nature Poetry*, with poems by John Sewell, Colin Sutherill, and Diana Syder (Redbeck Press, 1997).

Many of the poems in Part 1 were first written on leave of absence from Bretton Hall College of Leeds University to be Writer-in-Residence at Lenoir-Rhyne College, Hickory, North Carolina, USA for Spring semester 1997. To both institutions acknowledgements are due here, and to Rand Brandes for the invitation.

Friday Janry 10th [1806]... In the evening late Captain Clark & some of the party returned to the Fort. They informed us that they had been about 25 Miles along the Sea Coast, nearly a South course to see the Whale, expecting to get some of the Meat of it, and that they had to pass over rockey mountains, to get to the place where the whale lay, & that the Indians had showed them, to where a whale lay; which had been a long time Dead, which was on a very large Rock. It was about 105 feet long & every way proportionable.

The Journals of the Lewis & Clark Expedition, Vol 11, The Journals of Joseph Whitehouse, May 14, 1804 - April 2, 1806, London: University of Nebraska Press, 1997, p.411.

'Only now are we slowly realising that nature can be confined only by narrowing our own concepts of it, which in turn narrows us. That is why we came to see the whale.'

Robert Finch, 'Very Like a Whale', in S.H. Slovic and T.F. Dixon, **Being in the World,** New York: Macmillan, 1993 p.24.

*For the Giacominos
Jill, Larry, Mario, Caitlan and Nick
who first and always made us welcome
in their nest above the ocean in the Montara woods.*

CONTENTS

Part I: BUFFALO BILL'S WILD WEST

Bringing the Haggis to Billy Collins / 11
'The Poet's Hand' Exhibition / 12
A Poem for Amy's Van / 13
Thomas Wolfe Memorial House / 14
How to Shoo an Elk / 15
The Sea Lions of Pier 39 / 16
What Bashō Could Say in Three Lines / 17
Dorm Drumming in Price Village / 18
Roper's Monterey Pines / 20
The Sound of Stone / 21
Collecting Stars at Joshua Tree / 22
Not Nature Writing / 24
Second Chance / 26
Whale Watching with a Boy and a Goat / 27
Montara Meditation / 28

Part II: OIKOUMENE

Poland, October 1991
    I   First Journey / 31
    II   Why is no-one Jogging? / 32
    III A Drive Through Silesia / 34
    IV Tyniec / 35
    V   Return Journey / 36
At Tarn Hows / 37
A Field above Swaledale / 38
Why it's not possible to slip into Bradford / 39
Summer Love / 40
Pat's Webbed Feet / 41
The Hot-dog Bun Tree / 42
The Cat of the Acropolis / 43
Agia Irini / 44
Cretan Runners / 45
Agia Paraskevi / 46

Hunting the Dolmen of Haute Languedoc / 47
Cairo / 48
Castlerigg Revisited / 50
Inishmore / 51
Island Amulet / 52
Turner and Dali in the Mountains / 53
'Taylorgill Force' / 54
Dropping the Pot / 55
The Single Falling Stone / 56

PART I

'BUFFALO BILL'S WILD WEST and CONGRESS of ROUGH RIDERS of the WORLD

ACTUAL SCENES GENUINE CHARACTERS

TWICE DAILY NIGHT as LIGHT as DAY'

> 'One generation's West became another generation's Midwest or Upper South... Throughout his adult life Andrew Jackson (US President 1829-37) called himself a "westerner", and his avid supporters revelled in "Old Hickory's" regional identity.' (He had moved from North Carolina across the Appalachian Mountains to 'the log-cabin village of Nashville'.)
>
> C.A. Milner II, C.A. O'Connor and M.A. Sandweiss, **The Oxford History of the American West**, 1994, p.1.

BRINGING THE HAGGIS TO BILLY COLLINS

was harder than getting an elephant
to his village in upstate New York.

"You declared food. What food?
Ok, Ok. So what is a haggis?"

What is a haggis? It's what the Scots
eat on Burns' Night, the food of poetry,

an essential gift for a New York poet.
FoodandAg specialists gathered round.

"Hey, look at this? A vegetarian haggis!
Nope, never seen this critter before."

Whereas the Somers farmer who figured
an elephant might ease the work a little

and mailed his brother in Africa
to just send him one, was doing fine

with customs and the boat up the Hudson
until he started walking his critter

up the rural lanes of West Chester
and found crowds slowed him to a halt.

So being the man who invented
show business for the rest of us,

he walked the last lanes by night
with the first elephant in America

and holed up by day in a barn,
charging money to view nature's

marvellous invention. And stealing
the poet's local story like this

would be bad if it weren't bartered by
'the chieftan o' the puddin'-race'.

'THE POET'S HAND' EXHIBITION, NEW YORK PUBLIC LIBRARY

In the night the poets speak
to each other from their open
manuscripts: '...a Poet that doth drink
life/ As lesser men drink wine'
booms Ezra Pound's bold print
to Emily Brontë's tiny script
that shrinks away from any hint
of being observed by Thoreau's gift
for recording nature's rhythms
in regularly dipped brown ink.
Whitman's deep in his revisions,
while Marianne Moore can only think,
in a hand that's quite discrete,
to correspond with everyone
thanking them for having come,
even poets off the street.

A POEM FOR AMY'S VAN

would be written in chunky letters.
They would be white on black.
Its lines would
      bump along
            without quite
stalling
and its stanza spaces
would be punctuated with
the flower-head hand-prints
of naughty children.

It would have a [   ]
in its dashboard
through which live high songs
of melancholy melodies
would eat up the miles.

Its vast emptiness
would be that of a cathedral:
for those who have accepted
the challenge of the journey,
an experience for which words
are strangely unpronounceable.

About some things in this poem
it would be best not to ask.
Steel yourself to trust
the smile of its steering wheel,
the giggle of its gearbox,
its impulse to hug all other
poems, cars, trucks, sidewalks,
double yellow lines
of apparently ambiguous meaning.

                And the tail-light
                of this poem
                would be covered
                with tape on which
                there would be
                hand-printed
                the word
                RED.

THOMAS WOLFE MEMORIAL HOUSE, ASHEVILLE, N.C.
For Billy Collins

Kelly collects the critters
from the sad stained shirts
of Thomas Wolfe with a drowning
water vacuum. (The descendants
of carpet beetles and silverbacks
have outlived him by half a century.)
A young Textiles Conservator,
she wears white gloves so as not
to take them home. As we bend
towards the Scotch tape scraps
they are preserved in, her fringe
touches my high forehead. She's unaware
that it's a quarter of a century
since I felt a frisson like that.

I chase the tour downstairs past
the hall mirror his mother's
boarders gazed into. We glimpse
ourselves touring the home he never
wrote in, in the town that exiled him,
photograph ourselves on his porch
and can't stop talking about the bugs.

HOW TO SHOO AN ELK

'They kick out
forwards,' she said
with Canadian sincerity,
'then stamp on you
when you're on the ground.'

Leaving the Rockies
for the airport my driver
with the Cleopatra eyes
had pointed out an elk
'with a fine set of prongs'.

'I couldn't get in my house
once, for one standing there
right in front of the door.'
Her face crinkles over high
cheekbones as she smiles.

She has travelled solo
for a year in Asia
and Australia, just built
her own house and looks,
I'd say, about twenty-two.

'I'd detour a block
just to avoid them.
You can't shoo an elk.'
Her power is in knowing
the limits of her power.

THE SEA LIONS OF PIER 39 SAN FRANCISCO

are rafted up,
heads hung to sea,
sardines heaped on
four squares of toast.

They stink, sleep,
hoink, bite, change
sleek black skins
for drying brown,

flop out from under
each other, slop
into cool sea, cruise
the other croutons,

surface into a snoozing
face, one flipper up,
hook the tail on
deck and blubber down.

Ignoring cameras,
commentators, ice-creams,
sunscreens, jugglers,
rubbernecks only feet away,

roundabouts, shoot-outs,
fire-eaters, videos,
a human on a single
wheel catching knives,

they do not look up
to answer why it is
they started summering
six years ago

and they exercise
a certain dignified
discretion not to ask
why we are here.

WHAT BASHŌ COULD SAY IN THREE LINES

In the stillness of North Carolina's Linville Gorge
the river's roar rises to the walls of Shortoff Mountain.
It is always there, cutting, grading, taking and giving
to Lake James. Only the bear hunters know it closely
in this cold season. I hear it when I look down, turning
slowly on the rope-end like a chrysalis on a thread under
the overhang I've finally fallen off. I rest, let the river in,
then turn my mind to ways of butterflying out of this
dead-end. Lowered to the crack off left and I'm flying
on a different course, fumbling to find a state of grace.

How our lives are measured by love songs as we travel.
In the truck, country singers try for images of 'flowing
like a river from the mountains to the sea'. They know
their clichés give a playful sense of control. They sing,
'How can I miss you if you won't go away?'
Rednecks ready to redefine a dead-end, moving on
without that butterfly stuff. I've moved away a while
and I miss you. It's your birthday and I'm a continent
away.
You call back when you've opened my present, a mountain
painting. No need for us to say 'I love you' and we don't.

A friend picks me up to drive to dinner at the home
of a woman who hugs me as I hold out my hand.
On the drive home suddenly my friend is saying,
'to hear the words "I love you" from your life's partner –
that's what I haven't heard for two years, since
my wife died. It's hard, you know?' And I find myself
struggling to respond, wanting to say something
of what a mountain learns from a cold river, what a river gives
to a humbled mountain how the bear senses flash floods
and how the river finds its way onward, onward, onward.

DORM DRUMMING IN PRICE VILLAGE

finger light
head torch
palm flash
skin pulse
chest drum
heart clap

ratchet, ratchet, ratchet, ratchet it up
    to the light bubbling laughter of release

        outside   sleet stings
                        cars slow
                        hawk hunches
                        leaves warm
                        mice curl
                        dark bites

finger flash
palm pulse
skin torch
chest clap
heart drum
head light

fade, fade, fade, fade it out.
    No need to say 'That one was lost'

        where   fog hangs
                        ice holds
                        cars slide
                        worms curl
                        leaves warm
                        dark bites

flash palm
torch chest
light head
clap skin
drum finger
pulse heart

feel, feel, feel, feel the fire
    of shared playful making in winter

        when   friendships shrink
                      thoughts freeze
                      dogma hunches
                      closure holds
                      dark bites
                      leaves warm

                                          mice
                                          worms
                                          seeds

ROPER'S MONTEREY PINES

He looks up each day at dawn
at those tall, tall trees he loves
to live with and one day may
kill him and his wife, computer
and cats, perhaps, in his small
wooden house on the highest
ridge of the Oakland hills.

'My God,' he jokes, 'I could
be found one morning with a tree
across my chest!' Clearly,
he thinks there could be
worse ways to go. He survived
all those years of scary abseils
on the lonely walls of Yosemite,

his famous running pendulum
to hook his fingers in a far crack
then climb above his loop of rope,
and the crazy parties in Camp 4.
Now he lives with earthquakes
and fires. A solid puddle of metal
that was a car squats on his table –

relic of an Oakland inferno
that killed at least one friend.
Each big storm another tree
falls ('Missed us again!') and feeds
his fire, but he gives the dignity
of falling to the trees that may
outlast him and he cannot fell.

THE SOUND OF STONE

Hidden from the sun and other climbers
in the Hidden Valley, under a leaning
wall of chalked little ledges a single
taped voice echoes from the wooden
choirstalls and stone vaulted roof
of some European cathedral. I'm drawn
through the scent of the lone pinyon pine
and find this boy with battery-powered
tape-deck, slippers, shorts and chalk.
He is almost voiceless, speaks little
to my questions. Empty eyed, he's wintered out
here with the desert stones and Joshua trees.
He turns away to pump his traverse again,
panting so much he can't hear the calm
of this cathedral, its stilling single voice.

COLLECTING STARS AT JOSHUA TREE

First the comet's flaring tail
at 5 am. *'I used to pee in great arcs
before the war'*, Roper had quoted
last night. 'Now that's poetic!'
said Steck. Back in my bag
'Hale-Bopp, Hale-Bopp'
is a new mantra for sleep.

Woken by the howling of coyotes
close to camp and then, at dawn,
the cactus wren calling us to rise
with hats (and gloves in Kelsey's case
for walking dogs in the desert).
It's my first day at Joshua Tree –
'Ah, a virgin!' observes Roper.

So we begin with Mike's Books
where I grunt and sweat in the sun,
see snow on a far mountain
from the granite monolith's top.
Then Toe Jam to Lazy Day
(which isn't) and seeking shade
by now, Lickety Split's finger-locks.

The afternoon's light breeze allows
A Walk On The Wild Side, three
slab pitches of pressing granules
and crimping credit-card edges.
'Heels down!' shouts Roper above,
'And stand up like a man!' as I start.
Pitch two's traverse steepens. I'm off-

on-off-on and whimpering, apparently,
with effort. 'Don't scream, just fall!'
Roper's voice drifts down. 'Ah, full-
body friction, eh?' I slap for a ledge
and heave. Roper leads on until
the rope runs out. 'Don't fall,' he says
finally, braced in a bowl, unbelayed.

Next day at Dairy Queen Wall
all we see are ice-cream comets
shooting up: Scrumdillyshus has us
stemming into sky (Steck starts
with one shoe untied). Frosty Cone
has beautiful brackets to pinch
and Double Decker, steep delight.

In the shade of Hidden Valley
below Sail Away we meet travellers
collecting three-starred climbs
they name. 'And this one's like
champagne.' It is. We head back
for The Headstone's Left Edge.
On top I listen to desert silence,

see from above that these stones
are in circles enclosing space
as space encloses us and we
people it with names for stones.
During my last night committing
stars to memory, weekend stargazers
people the camp with telescopes.

On the drive out I accept
the totem gift of a Golden Eagle
atop a telegraph pole. On the flight
home to Hickory I see the night sky
in scattered farms and highways
as the ancients saw their land and
experience laid out above them.

NOT NATURE WRITING
For Gill

I

Tentless, stoveless, mapless
we leave for three days
Dave Mazel and me, lighting out
into the Bitterroot Mountains
like naive, excited kids
following a tale of a trail
Dave had heard back by the river
in Missoula where Barry Lopez
had read like a sage. I heard
the bugs are bad out there.

But, hey, we have bread
and cheese, salami and wine.
There's blue behind those
Montana thunderheads and water
springs clear from mossy holes
beside the path we finally lose
at a lake. We search around and return.
'How about we balance
across the log dam?' Dave's words
are better than Nature Writing.

There's a faint trail on the far
side and a view of a peak
like a layered iced cake.
'Wouldn't that make a noble
objective?' Dave has an ice-axe
and a language to match.
'Bushwhacking' is the only word
for our illiterate attempts to find
animal trails that read rock shelves
into a high basin, a grassy glade.

II

Now, I could tell you about
the lightening storm that night,
about my neolithic snow daggers,
a sudden wilderness of peaks,
the bull moose grazing through
his evening glade's willow fringe,
but even those ferocious
all dancing, all biting bugs
pale beside that moment when
I pulled from my sleeping bag

your shirt, that sleeveless blue
gingham thing that seemed
too small, frail, far away.
Even travelling light
into a wild, still, retreat
you were there, at the back
of my head as I looked out
and learned how to be attentive,
how to listen both ways,
get up and get down the mountain.

SECOND CHANCE
For Bob Winter

And when the mountains came,
squeezed up between tectonic plates,
before ice, before frost, before water,
they sang to each other in the raw colours
of the earth's mineral palette.

The air screamed its cold sky-scream
as deserts stretched themselves out
for the duration, not expecting the rains
which cut and crossed them towards
rising lakes of greens and deep blues.

And out of a lake, from its aeons
of chemical mutations and many deaths
of many species, there flew the first fish
again, wandering cautiously as if evolved
to avoid, this time, the growth of a brain.

WHALE WATCHING WITH A BOY AND A GOAT

"Check out the wild flowers", he says.
I bend over an orange trumpet vibrating
towards the sun from thin gravel and grass.
The goat, its lead slipped, does the same.
"Hey, a red tailed hawk!" Checking us out,
tilting, turning, the bird wobbles its spread
tail glowing like sunlit stained glass.

Coming over a rise the boy, trotting goat,
and I suddenly hear the ocean's deep throated
pounding in from Asia onto this Californian shore.
I am led down onto his headland like a child.
This boy of twelve is my guide to whale watching.
"Here's a coyote scat – that's a scientific word
for poop." I'm to look south for a spout, then
for another close behind, mother and calf passing
Shark Bay to summer, if they make it, off Canada.

My guide was off school sick, but before I set out
he came over O.K., needed fresh air. He wrestles
with the goat above the yellow foam-fingered bay
while I scan the green sea for a dark cruising
shape close in, or a fabled fountain far out.
The day passes like they do in California. Mist
closes over the hills up the coast. The sea breeze
chills. All the small flowers have been seen. Coffee
calls, back at his house in the woods. We head home.

The boy keeps waving me ahead. He slows to slower
than sauntering. A mile short of home I decide
he is ill, run ahead for his mother and the van
for the boy and the goat. He'd had the shits bad
and pooped his pants, guiding a stranger and all,
who had not even seen a whale. His mother smiled.
Next day I watched again: one spout, then another.

MONTARA MEDITATION

How soothing is the sea rolling onto rocks
at the end of its long trip across
the surface tensions of the globe.
Welcome, waves, to America!
I'm leaving tonight the surface smoothness
of America, migrating like the whales out there,
knowing the hidden battles being fought
and ignored in the name of Nature.

They think they've caught the Unabomber
who for fifteen years from his tiny cabin
cycled at dawn to post packages aimed
at academic explorers taking technology
too far. But not to eco-friendly UC Davis
where they built the sports hall too close
to the bank-holes of Burrowing Owls
they tried to preserve by posting 'Nature Reserve'.

Even John Muir's home is overrun
by the railroad he brought in to sell
his Royal Ann cherries. And here above the beach
of Montara, locals fight the road across the mountain.
I wear their 'Think Tunnel' T-shirt
heading home to unsolved riddles
like B.S.E. and Sellafield's waste.
Meanwhile I'm still learning to watch whales.

PART II: OIKOUMENE

The known land of the ancient and medieval world on the map of Johannes Eschuid (Venice, 1489).

POLAND, OCTOBER 1991

I
FIRST JOURNEY

There was opera on the train.
First the tape went wobbly,
then it went under the black scream
of this night express from Warsaw to Gliwice
which first hit the high note
then shook with vibrato
on rails made for freight.

Two youngish men lean forwards,
heads together,
exchanging lectures on points
made in the newspaper.
The first election for years
is eight days away.

In the buffet car the elderly waiter
has the all-suffering face
of patient, distant dignity.

He is the face of a nation,
of a generation,
of an old waiter
on a hurtling train
carrying the same people
towards the next future
and there is opera on the train.

II
WHY IS NO-ONE JOGGING?

It is Sunday afternoon
at the allotments of Gliwice,
dug in between the main road
flowing constantly with cars
and the river flowing swiftly
with raw sewage towards
the tower blocks of the town.

I am jogging with GREENPEACE
on my vest towards the chimneys
beyond the town, beyond the park,
dark with big trees, grass uncut,
where few families are walking.

I am jogging down the ash road
past the allotments' wire fences
and high gates. Hard to tell
how many families are here
among the fruit trees and huts,
a private home, a chimneyed house
you can call your own.

This is the family heirloom:
subsistence, retreat, but not
to turn potatoes out of earth
that is poisoned by pollution.
Resistance is in flowers!
Answer communism with cacti
in your greenhouse! Whilst they can
pickle fungi from the fields,
or harvest nuts from the woods,
they cannot eat the apple of bad air,
the fruit of their father's tree.

But here they could talk
without being overheard,
exchange jokes and seeds
of a green opposition
that in those days swelled
to things you could eat.

It is Sunday afternoon
at the allotments of Gliwice
and democracy has flowered
into so many heads
that no-one knows how many.
Several are Green
and hold the seeds
of unemployment, they are saying
here in the second homes.

III
A DRIVE THROUGH SILESIA

A man leads a heavily shod
Workhorse down a country road.
It is the ploughing season.
They plod along together
Towards his strip of field.
Later a tractor ploughs
As far as the flat grey sky.

A woman leads a cow by its chain
Through the village. Both black
And heavy, they swing along back
To the verge of the road.
One cow for the family,
Two more for the milk money.
Harvest is the season of TV sales.

We visit The Crag Under The Castle
Then The Crag Under The Forest
And I'm shown the secret of The Circus,
A high open-roofed bowl where there's
Been left a simple bracken bed.
Driving back we pass an industrial town
That poisons every season:

One in twenty babies will not live
To climb a crag or lead a cow.

IV
TYNIEC

Careering out of Cracow
chasing the last of the light
the car had to slow after the village
where the bends turned field-
corners and the headlights caught
a boy and a girl under a willow
just standing, a metre apart,
staring at this mad car.
It had to halt at the river.

And we all got out to stand
in the perfect stillness,
to smell the autumnal dusk,
to feel darkness falling
on the fields, the slouching river
and to look across, along the wire
of the now defunct ferry,
to a white crumbling monastery
perched on the brink of water and

night and the memory of
an atheist businessman,
a Cracow boy,
a returned self-exile
in a fast foreign car
who wanted to show us
this childhood place
where something had happened
and was happening now.

V
RETURN JOURNEY

An icy moon is tipped above
the first glow of dawn
as the frosted towns drift by:
Gliwice, Zabze, Katowice.
At each station the faces
of the old ones fill with tears
as they wave off furiously
their children and their children
after the All Saints Day visit.

Yesterday the old ones scrubbed
the tombs, polished the marble
of the graves of their parents
while the roads of the nation
throbbed, the railway lines pulsed
with the pull of family blood
back to the burial grounds.

After so many borders redrawn,
repatriation, insurrection,
and now the latest liberation,
the Poles returned last night
to the land of the dead.
Every cemetery was lit
by thousands of candles
clustered on the glinting tombs.

Amongst the heavy odour of
chrysanthemums in armfuls
arranged earlier on every grave,
the nation walked with its past,
stared together at the life
of the last generation,
revisited each year at
what the communists renamed
'The Festival of The Dead'
and can now be reclaimed
as 'All Hallows E'en'.

AT TARN HOWS, NEW YEAR'S DAY, 1996

They throw their voices across the ice
to hear the woods return their cries
out of a misted dignity of silence.

They think their shouted graffiti gives life
to this hibernating hollow in the mountains
which hugs its sap quietly into itself.

The foot-printed ice goes on thawing out
the tracks of these small creatures, hidden
on their circular pathways. The slightest light

of a distant sun sucks back the ice-mist.
The earth collapses underfoot, its frost-swell
empty, unmade by the season's gift.

But this species goes on making marks –
carparks, labels, signs – thinking that they made
this place, its magic, with a concrete dam.

A FIELD ABOVE SWALEDALE
For Izabel in Brazil

Driving up this high lane linking
Maske to Merrick, I summit and
suddenly the far moor's edge
is a perfect line across the dale.
Something is happening. I stop the car.
The sun set half an hour ago.

Towards dalehead, the sky is a chorus
of yellows reaching up and out
towards the tipped ear of the moon.
Do you hear it? Does that tilted
listening dish beam it back down
as the chorus of your summer dawn?

The sky overhead is a starless dome,
a dark hemisphere for earth-echoes
like the crunch of my boots across
this frosted field. Over the wall I watch
a hare, the power in her high haunches
bouncing her nose across the ground.

And look, another loping along behind,
pulled by this season's power of pairs.
Frost now nips my ears. The sky is orange,
warm and wide. The stars are out.
It could be almost dawn down there
up here, but for the silent moors.

WHY IT'S NOT POSSIBLE TO SLIP INTO BRADFORD

There is a point where you pause
in the sky for a moment,
before the motorway tips you
down into Bradford.

There is a place where wild
hill farms walled the moors in,
before those windy glass schools
and way before Morrison's.

This is the moment when
choices were made, when gravity
had men committed to Bradford
to do the deal right and return

alongside the river or back over
the rim, better or bettered, loaded
or light. Now you still notice
that something is happening

inside your head though your
journey flows on and freewheeling
into the city you realise that
somehow Bradford chose you.

SUMMER LOVE

He descended towards the dale
passing through the net
woven by sweeping swifts.

As though left by the retreat
of a lapping green sea,
lines of hay rippled below.

He pushed at the gate
down to her road, noticed
the usual squeak. Paused.

Could he tell her?

The swifts screamed their hurry
to be done before
the long pull of Africa.

The oystercatcher piped
from the river it would follow
to winter by the sea.

He had to go
to tell her
he had to go.

PAT'S WEBBED FEET

They said I lived on water when I was young.
Leaving my land life behind after the bell
I slipped my mooring and found my proper balance
under sail. I could read the wind across
a sheet of water, knew the maze of reedbeds,
dykes and reaches. The Broads, empty at evening,
were my Looking-Glass Land. An hour or two out
I'd try to lose myself, set the sail, slip down
into the bottom of the boat and stare at sky,
listen to the lap of water on the clinkers,
the courting cries of wildfowl, until a nudge
of mudbank told me it was time to tie up
and find the nearest church. A tower drew me to it
like a mast. But I'd want to leave my mark. Always
I'd sign the book then walk away to water once again,
until the summer in my sixteenth year. I'd drifted,
drifted into this church and sat too long.
It was getting dark. I found the fat leather
visitors' book, opened it and suddenly saw the flat
black body of a frog, its webbed feet spread
on the white page. That was the summer I sold the boat
and met a boy who had an old black dreamy car.
We found some lanes you wouldn't know were there.

THE HOT-DOG BUN TREE
for Rand, Beth and Blake

is small in its corner
under the high laurel hedge.
It trembles its rusty barbs,
its russet firework fountains
on the end of its iron stems.
It carries the colour of autumn
under the bright spring sky
reflecting light off Dublin Bay.
Its two crossed hot-dog buns
wedged between stem and branch
are white as flesh, soft as
armchair birdwatchers missing
their North Carolina chickadee,
their usual mockingbird,
and the cardinal of home.
An Irish blue tit feeds
on the buns, then flies up
and taps at the window,
defying boundaries of glass.

THE CAT OF THE ACROPOLIS

is soft and the colour of honey,
creeping between thick columns
she is at home with the rising heat,
the indolent guards, the insurgent feet
of tourists come to see big paws
that subdue horses screaming in stone
on the Parthenon's pediment frieze
in the dreams of a nation,
in the myth of a metropolis
walled off from the wilderness.

The cat of the Acropolis sits
in the sun by the marble steps
waiting to be stroked and stroked,
hunting on her mountain by moonlight
behind walls that exclude those
lean roaming dogs of Athens from
that wilderness of tower blocks,
clogged cars, screaming scooters,
the undreamt-of civilization
that is their modern metropolis.

AGIA IRINI
Crete, 1993

"Kuree! Kuree! Kuree!"
The honey buzzard alarm cries,
gliding across from woods to walls
of white rock snaking downwards.

Juniper, olive, oak, sweet chestnut,
a garden of cones and nuts,
centuries of harvesting and planting
the wild outreach of the village.

Goats tinkle through the trees,
a grazing of untuned random bells,
black bearded, milk swinging,
half wild hill-tough meat and hide.

Bees hover in at letter-boxed hives
stone-levelled, boulder-topped,
painted pink, and blue edged,
a terraced row of honey-makers.

Here the village negotiates with nature,
taking and giving where summer's water
has dried back up to its spring
leaving this gorge empty and full,

the seasonal village trader's trail
from the White Mountains to the sea.
This year the first coaches come, taking
tourist crowds where the buzzard cries.

CRETAN RUNNERS
Gerakari, 22 August 1994

He goes to the mirror in the back of the café
and rewinds the white fringe of 'tears'
that is his tasselled sweatband. He tucks
a red blossom behind his ear, lifts
an elbow for my photograph of the mirror,

proud to be racing the 10 K today
wearing this reminder of his family's
resistance to the Turks. Like nervous bees
the runners swarm up and down the street.
A joker jogs out of the café, prancing

in his new deck shoes. Sudden springs
of heel-slapping bring cheers from the crowd.
An old man in breeches, boots and black 'tears'
makes his way across the street to ask Gill
if she is German. The church bells strike eleven

and still nothing happens. The runners suggest
as starting line a recent road repair.
Gun in the air, a man saunters down the street
and shoots as he walks. The police car picks up
the winded children at the foot of the first hill.

And down the Amari valley they unwind
a Cretan celebration of resistance that survived
the massacre of mountain men fifty years ago.
At Vrises the war memorial is a feeding station.
In Drigies it flutters with Greek flags.

At Ano Meros, when we arrive, the runners
each clutch a laurel branch, glowing with sweat,
smiles and stories, the feasting and dancing still to come,
only the lament of the Svakion anthem
a reminder of the absence of men growing old.

AGIA PARASKEVI
for Evie and Malcolm

The buzzard's cry, of pain or desire,
echoes above the olive groves.

The smell of the pig snoring under
the olives is a wall to walk through.

The sawing of the donkey straining
at his circle round an olive root

is the sound of double service:
dung for the far field and

a driver's comfort, single stirupped,
bringing green leaves from the field

to the milk goat and her kid
fenced under the olive grove.

At night the koukouvayies play
their two note duet, high and low,

she and he, always urgent, always
distant, over the olive groves.

By night, under the vines, the villagers
eat with the smooth oil of the olives.

But beyond the village, over the gully
where her icon was found, they built

on a bridge, a small church
to Saint Friday, Agia Paraskevi,

who heals eyes, for not to see
is not to work, to live a half-life

of sounds and smells, eating and drinking
away the slow years of the olive groves.

HUNTING THE DOLMEN OF HAUTE LANGUEDOC

I pause on the first bend
Out of the village and study
The stillness deep in the gorge.
Only the martins move through it.

The last of the morning mists
Of Haute Languedoc are fading fast
On horizon beyond horizon. Still
Everything sleeps under the sun.

Cycling shirtless up the bends
Where light passes through
The pale dry grassheads, I scan
Shrubbed limestone pavement

For the lifted flat stone,
The old form, its gravity
Defining the elements: sky
And earth held in balance.

Those who raised this old magic
In this high, wide place possessed
A certainty that still can
Stagger me at first view.

My frail bicycle wheels spin
As I lay my machine to rest
And confront a stone culture
That must have also known

The ways of water, sun and wind
Upon their white shellrock: that
The river dries back underground
Differently each generation,

That the cave collapses and
The very rock is remnant –
There is no permanence.
But this is our certainty.

CAIRO
For Fred

"Take it easy sir. This is Cairo.
No accidents." My foot twitches to the floor
again and my eyes are closed to the secret
that everyone gives way, finally.

Unseen on the roofs of these teeming
tower blocks a million people live
the village life they've left behind,
their hens and rabbits in crude hutches.

High in my hotel I watch wild
parakeets flock from palm to palm
in the zoo gardens below, not daring
to step out on the street of beggars,

helpers, dust and smog. Islamic terrorists
are moving about below under those trays
of oranges, big cloth bundles, furniture.
Cairo from the air. To take a walk seems

naive. I ring my only Arab friend.
Her husband is away but her brother
might be able to come with us. She wants
to show me the pyramids. Her boy brings

his football. Suddenly it's there, The Great
Pyramid, rising behind the houses
of a Cairo street, huge and sad
like the camel that accosts me, crossing

and recrossing my path, its smiling
driver half pleading, half insisting
as his father did to my father
only half a century ago.

In Egypt, persistence pays. Ask
the makers of pyramids by the dozens
and the buried sun boat, elegantly
built, full size, for use in eternity.

Ask the carvers of kings, the packers
of tombs, the bakers of clay messages.
Ask the chisellers of hieroglyphs
around the rims of granite coffins.

Ask the fly around the nose of
Edward Said that seemed to be
in better shape than he was.
"In Egypt, our present we live
as history." Ask the chiseller
on the Cairo University desk
whose history is poignantly present
in these eloquent hieroglyphs:

'Hany is my love
                  Glad
23/11/91
Together forever'

About Egypt, persistence is what
I came to comprehend. Ask the waiter
who tried to move us *inside* the Sheraton
from the floating tables where the Nile

divides and a winter wind had us hunched
up but determined to see out the sunset.
"We like it here," my Californian friend
half lies, "and sunsets we understand."

CASTLERIGG REVISITED

Mute stones for telling seasons
speak to Gore-tex and Leica
about time and distance and wind
from which this species is now
protected, just as it protects
grass with erosion control,
making a wicker basket of eggs,
a taped off family of stones,
a corral of grass growing back
to the required standard as if
only rocks ever lived here,
fallen from heavens they know
but speak of no longer.

INISHMORE

So finally, backs to the sea,
they walled themselves in,
here where good green earth
dreams a black jaw foaming,
its roar constant under the wind's edge.

Backs to the storms' salt spray
they rolled grey rocks into tight
chainmail, semi-circling themselves,
their potatoes, their goats,
their smoke-dark turf huts.

And next summer they started again,
rolling, levering, raising,
the outer circle confirming
their confidence here between
the weather and the walls.

So now, backs to the cosmos,
we remain between walls
and warming weather, musing
and musing on how to reverse
the outer circle we've made.

ISLAND AMULET

The island's tourists savour the flesh of fresh salmon
The island's salmon swim at the head of the loch
At the head of the loch the tides barely reach
Where the tides barely reach the salmon cages float
Towards the caged salmon flesh swim the sea lice
Against the sea lice the farmer feeds ivermectin
Ivermectin the toxic loves the flesh of the mussels
The flesh of the mussels is loved by the tourists
Few tourists at first suffer shellfish poisoning
Shellfish poisoning is killing more island tourists
The island's tourists savour the flesh of fresh salmon.

TURNER AND DALI IN THE MOUNTAINS

Turner's mobile phone
was always switched off,
the net was down,
even his faxes,
those old delicate
pencil on paper memos,
printed out fuzzy.

It did not need Dali
to hang on a pastoral
pitchfork (conspicuously climbed
by the snail of death)
a telephone, its wire cut,
to define a 'Mountain Lake'.

For Turner there was only
out there, in your face,
chaos theory of colour,
post-pastoral clashing of rocks
and counter-angled clouds,
wet always on the way,
flowing, breaking, leaping,
leaning on in towards
the painter, one of those naive
small mortals, mysterious
in the business of living
with tiny boats, bony cows,
dwarfed sheep, a metal-clasped,
leather-bound sketchbook.

On blue paper,
pen, ink and chalk
could say all this.
For Turner the phone
was already cut off.

'TAYLORGILL FORCE, SEATHWAITE' BY IAN WALTON

And the more he looked
the more he heard only
that far fall of narrow light
where the whole sky's rain
was funnelled into a glittering
roar, the single iridescent voice
of the dark fell, its deep woods
and silent walls, until, still staring
and staring, there came out of the gloom
this nearer, frailer, higher sound
of water wearing its way through the land
as if lit by a last touch of sun
for barely a moment
before night closed upon
Taylorgill Force,
the sky cutting a mountain

DROPPING THE POT
For Jack Blackburn

'See,' he says, 'the way the heat has swept
up the pot, the dusting of ash low down,
the discrete application of salt, the trick
of not letting the glaze run all the way

down, this salmon pink that comes only
from the firing.' He finds the French potter's
words: 'Raku yields so as to gain tension.'
Thumb in a Virot bowl, he lifts it

casually, like an old friend, swirls
his other hand around it, saying, ' see
the glaze is like a woman's diaphanous
dress, whereas the black raku is masculine,

built up, layer upon layer on white clay.'
'But what', I ask, 'if you drop one?'
'In June', he says, 'I dropped the coffee pot
of a potter who'd died in February.

I was rushing and it broke to smithereens.
It was expensive, but they are for using.
I grieved for that pot, but at least
dropping the pot meant something.'

THE SINGLE FALLING STONE
i.m. Paul Nunn

Whenever I take the longest drive north
and west at Whitsun I think of Nunn other
than a name that echoes through the guidebook
like his laugh, the indoor bagpipes
of the climbing village, slightly embarrassing
needing all the space of Peakland moors,
Sutherland, the Karakoram: 'as the mountain valleys
open up one feels that one is coming home.'

Outlandish, like those obscure scraps
of facts he'd pin you down with while
he built a theory between one pint and the next
he'd always offer anyone at hand. Such hands
you'd think grasped summits annually, yet
how often he'd return empty handed home
from home. 'We had no commitments, except
to ourselves, and they were satisfied.'

He'd lost friends to the single falling stone,
the sudden moment of snow slide, serac crack
we must struggle to accept. 'Some day soon
some must fall. It was a case of grinning
and ignoring them.' Out here, where sea
and mountains meet, where the sky's big-hearted,
something is missing and present between sun
and showers in his 'far far away land'.